11/08

U.S. Sites and Symbols

Seals

Annalise Bekkering

WEIGL PUBLISHERS INC.

Published by Weigl Publishers Inc.
350 5th Avenue, Suite 3304, PMB 6G
New York, NY 10118-0069

Website: www.weigl.com
Copyright ©2009 WEIGL PUBLISHERS INC.

Library of Congress Cataloging-in-Publishing Data

Bekkering, Annalise.
 Seals / Annalise Bekkering.
          p. cm. – (U.S. sites and symbols)
 Includes index.
 ISBN 978-1-59036-893-0 (soft cover: alk. Paper)—ISBN 978-1-59036-892-3 (hard cover: alk. Paper) 1. Seals (Numismatics)—United States—States—Juvenile literature. I. Title.
 CD5603.B45 2009
 929.90973—dc22

2008015828

Printed in the United States of America
1 2 3 4 5 6 7 8 9 0 12 11 10 09 08

Editor: Danielle LeClair
Designer: Kathryn Livingstone

Photograph Credits
Weigl acknowledges Vector-Images.com, Shutterstock, and Dreamstime as the primary image suppliers for this title. Unless otherwise noted, all images herein were obtained from Vector-Images.com, Shutterstock, Dreamstime, and their contributors.

Every reasonable effort has been made to trace ownership and to obtain permission to reprint copyright material. The publishers would be pleased to have any errors or omissions brought to their attention so that they may be corrected in subsequent printings.

Contents

What are Symbols?

A symbol is an item that stands for something else. Objects, artworks, or living things can all be symbols. Every U.S. state has official symbols, or emblems. These items represent the people, history, and culture of the state. State symbols create feelings of pride and citizenship among the people who live there. Each of the 50 U.S. states has an official seal. It is called the state seal.

Seals have been used since ancient times. Early middle eastern cultures used seals in 3200 BC to authenticate clay tablets. Seals were also used in ancient Egypt, Greece, and Rome. In China and Japan, seals were used to identify possessions. The use of seals in England dates back to 7th century royalty. England's King John used the first "Great Seal" in the 13th century for his personal documents. The tradition of adding a seal to official documents was brought to the United States with colonists. Some state seals were brought to the United States from England. Others were developed when the states were still territories or achieved statehood.

Many early seals were made by dripping hot wax onto a document and pressing a form, often a ring, into the wax.

Finding State Seals by Region

Alaska

Hawai'i

Washington

Montana

Oregon

Idaho

Wyoming

The West

Nevada

Utah

Colorado

California

Arizona

New Mexico

Each state has a seal. In this book, the states are ordered by region. These regions are the West, the Midwest, the South, and the Northeast. Each region is unique because of its land, people, and wildlife. Throughout this book, the regions are color coded. To find a state seal, first find the state using the map on this page. Then, turn to the pages that are the same color as that state.

North Dakota
Minnesota
Wisconsin
Michigan

South Dakota
Iowa

The Midwest

Nebraska
Illinois
Indiana
Ohio

Kansas
Missouri
Kentucky

West Virginia
Virginia

New York
Pennsylvania

The Northeast

New Hampshire
Vermont
Maine
Massachusetts

Rhode Island
Connecticut
New Jersey
Delaware
Maryland

Oklahoma
Arkansas
Tennessee
North Carolina

South Carolina

The South

Georgia

Texas
Alabama
Mississippi
Louisiana
Florida

Web Crawler

Find out facts about each state at
www.americaslibrary.gov. Click on
"Explore the States."

The West

The West is made up of 13 states. They are Alaska, Arizona, California, Colorado, Hawai'i, Idaho, Montana, Nevada, New Mexico, Oregon, Utah, Washington, and Wyoming. Alaska is far to the north. It is separated from the rest of the country by Canada. The Pacific Ocean borders Alaska, Washington, Oregon, and California, and surrounds Hawai'i.

Colorado

Arizona

Hawai'i

The West has many different landforms. There are glaciers in Alaska and volcanoes on Hawai'i. Giant redwood forests grow in Oregon. Deserts cover parts of Arizona, California, Nevada, and Utah. The Rocky Mountains run through Alaska, Washington, Idaho, Montana, Wyoming, Utah, Colorado, and New Mexico.

About 65 million people live in the West. American Indians, Asians, Hispanics, and people of British and German backgrounds make up the largest cultural groups. Nearly four million people live in Los Angeles, California. It is the region's largest city.

Alaska

Web Crawler

Trace important events in the history of the West at **www.pbs.org/ weta/thewest/events**.

Discover the West's natural wonders by clicking on the states at **www.nps.gov**.

California

Alaska

Alaska's seal was created in 1910. It became the official state seal in 1959 when Alaska became a state. Alaska's seal represents the state's abundant natural resources. Images of a farmer, horse, and wheat show the value of Alaska's agriculture. Ships portray the importance of sea transportation. Other resources important to Alaska are mining, rail transportation, forestry, and marine wildlife. The seal also depicts Alaska's natural beauty.

Arizona

Arizona's seal was adopted in 1911. The seal features major industries in Arizona. A **reservoir** and dam are depicted in the background. Fields of cotton and orchards, and an image of cattle symbolize the importance of agriculture. A quartz mine is shown on the left-hand side with a miner. Above the images are the words *Ditat Deus*. This is Arizona's state motto which means "God enriches" in Latin.

California

California's seal was adopted in 1849. It features Minerva, the Greek goddess of wisdom. At her feet, grapes and grain represent the state's agricultural richness, and the bear represents California's wildlife. *Eureka* is a Greek word, meaning "I have found it." This refers to the California Gold Rush. Ships are shown on the Sacramento River, flowing among the Sierra Nevada Mountains.

Colorado

Colorado's seal was adopted in 1877. It features the eye of God within a triangle. Below the eye is a bundle of sticks, held together with bands labeled "Union and Constitution." The sticks represents strength in unity. The mountains and the miner's tool symbolize the state's natural resources. The motto *Nil Sine Numine* is Latin for "nothing without the **deity**."

Hawai'i

The rising Sun on Hawai'i's seal represents the birth of a new state. The seal, adopted in 1959, features King Kamehameha the Great and the goddess of liberty holding Hawai'i's state flag. A **phoenix** symbolizes the change from a **monarchy** to democracy. Along the bottom of the seal is Hawai'i's state motto, *Ua Mau ke Ea o ka Aina I ka Pono*. This means "the life of the land is **perpetuated** in righteousness."

Idaho

Idaho has the only state seal designed by a woman. In 1891, Emma Edwards won $100 in a contest to design Idaho's seal. A farmer and grain represent Idaho's vast agricultural resources. A miner and ore symbolize the mining industry, and trees stand for the timber industry. Mountains and streams symbolize the natural beauty of Idaho. A man and woman standing side by side signify equality.

Montana

Montana's seal was adopted in 1893. In the foreground, the seal features a plow, pickaxe, and miner's shovel. These symbolize agriculture and mining. Montana's abundance of gold and silver led to its nickname the "Treasure State." The words *oro y playa* are Spanish for "gold and silver." Mountains and the waterfalls of the Missouri River represent Montana's natural beauty.

Nevada

Nevada's state seal was adopted in 1866. It has 36 stars in the ring around its center. This shows that Nevada was the 36th state to enter the Union. A silver miner and a quartz mill on the seal represent mining. A steam train and telegraph poles symbolize transportation and communication. Wheat, a sickle, and a plow stand for Nevada's agriculture. Snow-peaked mountains span the background of the seal.

New Mexico

The New Mexico seal was designed in 1851 and adopted in 1912. A bald eagle symbolizes bravery, skill, and strength. Protected by the wings of the bald eagle is a Mexican brown eagle. It stands for the Mexican Republic.

Oregon

On Oregon's seal, a British ship is sailing away. This signifies the end of Great Britain's influence in Oregon. An American ship sails towards the land, representing America's independence and power.

Utah

Utah's seal features a beehive. Qualities of a beehive are industry, hard work, thrift, stability, and self-reliance. These values were very important to Utah's settlers.

Washington

Washington's seal features the image of George Washington. In 1889, a jeweler named George Talcott was asked to engrave an elaborate landscape scene for Washington's state seal. He thought that a simple design would be better. Talcott put an image of George Washington in the center. This design was accepted as Washington's official state seal.

Wyoming

Wyoming was the first government to grant equal rights to women. The center of the state seal features a woman holding a banner that says "Equal Rights." The pillars around the woman have banners that show the main industries in the state. A miner and a famer stand beside each pillar. The year 1869 is when Wyoming became a territory, and 1890 is when it became a state. The seal was approved in 1893.

The Midwest

The Midwest is in the center of the United States. It lies between the Rocky Mountains in the west and the Appalachian Mountains in the northeast. The Ohio River separates the Midwest from the South. Canada lies to the north. There are 12 states in the Midwest. They are Illinois, Indiana, Iowa, Kansas, Michigan, Minnesota, Missouri, Nebraska, North Dakota, Ohio, South Dakota, and Wisconsin.

Ohio

South Dakota

Illinois

The area from North Dakota to Missouri is made up of mostly farming states. They are part of the **Great Plains**. The states from Minnesota to Ohio border the Great Lakes. This chain of freshwater lakes acts as a border between the United States and Canada.

Nearly 65 million people live in the Midwest. There are large groups of African Americans, American Indians, and people of European descent. Many people live in cities. Chicago is the largest city in the Midwest. It is home to three million people. Chicago and other Midwest cities are known for blues, jazz, rap, and rock.

Indiana

Web Crawler

Discover the wildlife of Illinois at
http://dnr.state.il.us/lands/education/kids/toc.htm.

Explore a virtual Midwest farmhouse at
www.pbs.org/ktca/farmhouses/vf.html.

Iowa

Illinois

Illinois became a state on August 26th, 1818, and the state seal was adopted in 1868. Both these dates are displayed on the state seal. An eagle carries a shield with 13 stars and stripes that represents the original 13 states. In its beak, the eagle carries a banner that reads "State, **Sovereignty**, National Union."

Indiana

Indiana's seal features a buffalo jumping over a log and a woodsman chopping down a sycamore tree. In the background, the Sun sets over the hills. The border of the seal features leaves of the tulip tree, Indiana's state tree. The year 1816 refers to the year Indiana became a state. A version of this seal has been used since 1801.

Iowa

Iowa became a state in 1846. Iowa's seal was created in 1847. It features industries and natural resources of Iowa. A cultivator in a wheat field lies in front of a steamboat traveling down the Mississippi River. A soldier stands in the wheat field holding an American flag. An eagle holds a banner with the state motto "Our liberties we prize, and our rights we will maintain."

Kansas

Kansas's state seal was adopted in 1861. The seal has 34 stars, representing Kansas becoming the 34th state on January 29, 1861. Above the stars, the motto *Ad astra per aspera* is Latin for "to the stars through difficulty." The economy of Kansas is represented by a steamboat on a river, a farmer plowing a field, and a settler's cabin. Behind the field are ox wagons. In the background, American Indians are hunting buffalo.

Michigan

Michigan's seal was adopted in 1835.

An American eagle represents the United States. The eagle is holding an olive branch, which is a symbol of peace. An elk and a moose hold a shield symbolizing Michigan's wildlife. The shield features a man with his hand raised in peace. *E Pluribus Unum* is Latin for "From many, one." *Tuebor* means "I will defend." *Si Quaris Peninsulam Ampanam Circumspice* means "If you seek a pleasant peninsula, look about you."

Minnesota

The Sun rises over the plains on Minnesota's seal, representing the landscape of the

state. An American Indian on horseback symbolizes Minnesota's heritage. A farmer and a tree stump represent Minnesota's industries and economy. In the background, the Mississippi River and St. Anthony Falls signify the importance of waterways for transportation.

Missouri

Missouri's seal features two grizzly bears, which symbolize strength and bravery, holding a shield. The shield contains a bald eagle on one side, representing the United States. On the other side, there is a grizzly bear and a crescent moon, which symbolized Missouri's small population when it became a state. Missouri's state motto, *Salus Populi Suprema Lex Esto,* is Latin for "Let the welfare of the people be the supreme law."

Nebraska

The main themes of Nebraska's seal are transportation, industry, settlement, and agriculture. A train travels towards the Rocky Mountains, and a steamboat moves through the Missouri River. A cabin, cornfields, wheat, and a blacksmith represent the importance of settlers and industry. The seal was adopted in 1867, the same year Nebraska became a state.

North Dakota

North Dakota's seal represents the state's landscape, natural resources, and history. The state tree, the American elm, stands in the middle of the seal. Bundles of wheat, a plow, and an anvil refer to the state's vast agricultural resources. An American Indian on horseback hunts a buffalo, representing North Dakota's culture and history. The emblem was approved as the territorial seal in 1863, and North Dakota became a state seal in 1889.

Ohio

Ohio's seal portrays the state's landscapes. The Sun radiates over Mount Logan in the background. The Scioto River separates the mountain from flat fields of wheat. Thirteen rays of Sun symbolize Ohio's 13 original colonies, while the wheat shows the importance of agriculture. A bundle of 17 arrows represent Ohio as the 17th state to join the Union. Ohio's current seal was adopted in 1996.

South Dakota

South Dakota's seal features the diversity of its economy and resources. A furnace symbolizes mining. The farmer and herd of cattle show the importance of agriculture to the state. A steamboat travels over the river, representing transportation. The seal was adopted in 1885, before South Dakota became a state in 1889.

Wisconsin

Wisconsin's seal features a sailor and a farmer holding a shield.

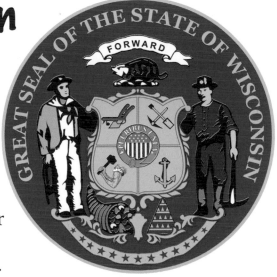

The shield represents four major sources of labor in the state—a plow for agriculture, a pickaxe for mining, an arm and hammer for manufacturing, and an anchor for fishing and shipping industries. Wisconsin is known as the "badger state." For this reason, a badger sits above the shield. Wisconsin's state motto, "Forward," is above the badger.

The South

The South is made up of 16 states. They are Alabama, Arkansas, Delaware, Florida, Georgia, Kentucky, Louisiana, Maryland, Mississippi, North Carolina, Oklahoma, South Carolina, Tennessee, Texas, Virginia, and West Virginia. The Atlantic Ocean borders the South from Delaware to the tip of Florida. A part of the Atlantic Ocean called the Gulf of Mexico stretches from Florida's west coast to Texas. Mexico lies to the south.

Florida

Alabama

Texas

The South is known for its warm weather. It also has plenty of rain. This makes it easy for plants to grow. In the past, cotton, tobacco, rice, and sugarcane were important crops in the South. They shaped southern history.

More than 100 million people live in the South. About 20 million are African American. Many people of Hispanic and European backgrounds also live there. Together, southerners share a special history and culture. Blues, gospel, rock, and country music all began in the South. Many well-known writers, such as Tennessee Williams, have lived there. The South is also known for its barbeque, Tex-Mex, and Cajun cooking.

West Virginia

Web Crawler

Read about the history of the South at **www.factmonster.com/ipka/A0875011.html**.

Explore the fun facts about the Southern states at **www.emints.org/ethemes/resources/ S00000575.shtml**.

Mississippi

Alabama

The seal of Alabama features a map of the state. The map shows Alabama's major rivers and the surrounding states. This seal was originally adopted in 1819, when Alabama first became a state.

Arkansas

Arkansas's seal features symbols of industry and agriculture on a shield in the center. An angel with the word "Mercy" and a sword with the word "Justice" surround the shield.

Delaware

Delaware's seal contains images of a farmer, a soldier, and the shipping industry. Delaware's state motto, "Liberty and Independence" is below the images.

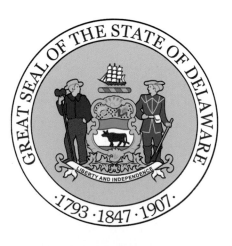

Florida

Florida's seal features a rising Sun, the state tree, a sabal palm tree, an American Indian woman scattering flowers, and a steamboat on water. The seal was initially adopted in 1868, with some changes made in 1985.

Georgia

Georgia's seal has an arch, supported by three pillars. The pillars represent three branches of government, which are legislature, judicial, and executive. The motto, "Wisdom, Justice, and Moderation," hangs from the pillars.

Kentucky

Kentucky's seal features a man dressed in buckskin and a man in formal clothes shaking hands. The man in buckskin represents the frontier, and the formally dressed man stands for the British coming to Kentucky.

Louisiana

Louisiana's seal features a pelican, the state's official bird. The pelican is caring for three chicks in a nest. The birds are surrounded by the state motto "Union, Justice, Confidence." The seal was adopted in 1902.

Maryland

Maryland's seal features a fisherman and a farmer on either side of a shield, with the Calvert family coat of arms. The design is based on a seal brought from England in the 1600s.

Mississippi

The seal of Mississippi features an American eagle. In its talons, the eagle holds an olive branch, representing peace. It also holds a quiver of arrows, symbolizing the power to go into battle.

North Carolina

North Carolina's motto, *Esse Quam Videri* is located at the foot of the seal. This motto is Latin for "To be, rather than to seem." The seal features the goddesses of liberty and of plenty. The state seal has changed many times. The current seal was created in 1983.

Oklahoma

Adopted in 1905, Oklahoma's seal displays a five-pointed star in the center. Each point of the star contains a symbol representing five American Indian Nations within the state. The central figure of two men shaking hands represents equality and justice between all people. The words *Labor Omnia Vincit* mean "Labor Conquers All Things." Forty-five small stars surround the large star. Oklahoma was the 46th state to enter the union in 1907.

South Carolina

South Carolina's seal contains two main images. The left image is of two palmetto trees—one standing, and one fallen. This scene represents a battle. The fallen tree stands for the British who were defeated. The motto *Quis Separabit* means "Who will separate?" The other image is a woman walking along a beach covered in weapons. She represents hope. The motto *Dum Spiro Spero* means "While I breathe, I hope." The seal was adopted in 1776.

Tennessee

The state seal of Tennessee was originally approved in 1796. The roman numerals XVI represent Tennessee as the 16th state to enter the United States in 1796. A plow, wheat, and a cotton plant signify the importance of agriculture to the state. A boat indicates the importance of shipping to the state's business and trade.

Texas

A five-pointed star is the central image in Texas's seal. A live oak branch and an olive branch are on either side of the star. The oak branch stands for strength, and the olive branch represents peace.

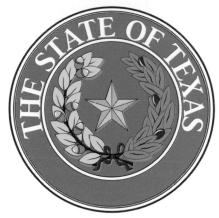

Virginia

The Roman goddess Virtus, the goddess of virtue, appears on Virginia's seal. The goddess represents heroism, righteousness, freedom, and valor. The state motto, *Sic Semper Tyrannis,* means "Thus always to tyrants."

West Virginia

The seal of West Virginia contains the motto *Montani Semper Liberi.* This is Latin for "Mountaineers are always free." The seal was adopted in 1863.

The Northeast

The Northeast is the smallest region in the United States. It is east of the Great Lakes and south of Canada. The Atlantic Ocean borders the Northeast coast. There are nine states in the Northeast. They are Connecticut, Maine, Massachusetts, New Hampshire, New Jersey, New York, Pennsylvania, Rhode Island, and Vermont.

Connecticut

Vermont

Maine

Many natural wonders are found in the Northeast. The Appalachian Mountains stretch through Maine, New Hampshire, Vermont, New York, and Pennsylvania. Lake Erie and Lake Ontario border New York. Niagara Falls flows between them. Half of Niagara Falls is located in the United States. The other half is located in Canada. On the U.S. side, the falls are 1,000 feet wide and 167 feet tall.

In the 1600s, the first settlers from Europe came to the area known as **New England**. Today, 55 million people live in the Northeast. More Irish Americans and Italian Americans live here than in any other part of the country. More than eight million people live in New York City, the largest city in the country.

New York

Web Crawler

Learn more about New England at **www.discovernewengland.org**.

See spectacular views of Niagara Falls at **www.niagarafallsstatepark.com/Destination_ PhotoGallery.aspx**.

Pennsylvania

Connecticut

The main features of Connecticut's seal are three grapevines that represent the three original colonies of the state. Beneath the grapevines, a banner contains the state motto, *Qui Transtulit Sustinet*. This means, "He who transplants still sustains." The original colonial seal was brought from England in 1639. It became the state seal in 1784.

Maine

Maine's seal was adopted in 1820. This was the same year Maine achieved statehood. Symbols on the seal represent the natural beauty, resources, and industry in Maine. On the shield, a moose rests under a pine tree. A farmer and a sailor stand on either side of the shield. The North star is at the top of the seal, with the motto *Dirigo* underneath. This means "I lead."

Massachusetts

An American Indian man is the central figure on Massachusetts' seal. He holds a bow and arrow. The arrow points down as a symbol of peace. A star over his right shoulder represents Massachusetts being one of the first 13 states. A Latin motto is written on a banner underneath the shield. *Ense petit placidam dub libertate quietem* means "By the sword we seek peace, but peace only under liberty." This became the official state seal in 1885.

New Hampshire

New Hampshire's seal was created in 1931. The ship *Raleigh*, one of the American Navy's first ships, is in the center of the seal. *Raleigh* was built in Portsmouth in 1776. It was the first ship to carry the American flag in battle. New Hampshire is known as the "Granite State." On the seal, a granite boulder is shown in the foreground. Laurel leaves surround the picture.

New Jersey

New Jersey became a state in 1776, and the state seal was adopted in 1777. The goddesses of liberty and grain are pictured on New Jersey's seal. Between them, a shield contains three plows, signifying the importance of agriculture to the state. The state animal, a horse, stands for speed and strength. A knight's helmet represents sovereignty. A banner at the bottom of the shield displays the state's motto, "Liberty and Prosperity."

New York

New York's state seal features two female figures, Liberty and Justice, standing on either side of a shield. The shield features New York's industry and natural resources. Two ships on a river travel in front of mountains. An American eagle sits above the shield, atop a globe showing the Atlantic Ocean. Under the shield, the motto *Excelsior* means "Ever upward." The seal was adopted in 1882.

Pennsylvania

Pennsylvania's seal was officially adopted in 1790. It features wheat, a ship, and a plow that represent the importance of agriculture and trade to the state.

Rhode Island

The seal of Rhode Island was adopted in 1644. The anchor is the main feature of Rhode Island's state seal. The word "Hope" is on a banner above the anchor.

Vermont

Vermont's seal features the state's natural beauty and resources. Wheat and a cow represent agriculture. The original seal was created in 1778. In 1821, a more complex seal was designed. In 1937, the state once again decided to use the original design.

The Great Seal

National emblems are symbols that are used for the entire country. The American flag, known as the star-spangled banner, is one such symbol. Another is the bald eagle, which is the the national bird. The oak tree is the national tree. The official seal of the United States is the Great Seal.

The Great Seal was finalized and approved on June 20, 1782. The seal reflects the Founding Fathers' beliefs and values of freedom and hope for the future for all Americans.

The first document to display the Great Seal was an agreement between George Washington and the British for better treatment of war prisoners.

The Great Seal is used about 2,000 to 3,000 times a year on official government documents.

History of the Great Seal

On July 4, 1776, Benjamin Franklin, John Adams, and Thomas Jefferson were asked to create a seal for the United States. The delegates of the Constitutional Convention believed an emblem and national coat of arms would show an independent nation and a free people with goals and grand hopes for the future.

Guide to State Seals

THE NATIONAL SEAL
Adopted: 1782

ALABAMA
Adopted: 1819

ALASKA
Adopted: 1959

ARIZONA
Adopted: 1911

ARKANSAS
Adopted: 1864

CALIFORNIA
Adopted: 1849

COLORADO
Adopted: 1877

CONNECTICUT
Adopted: 1784

DELAWARE
Adopted: 1777

FLORIDA
Adopted: 1868

GEORGIA
Adopted: 1798

HAWAI'I
Adopted: 1959

IDAHO
Adopted: 1891

ILLINOIS
Adopted: 1868

INDIANA
Adopted: 1801

IOWA
Adopted: 1846

KANSAS
Adopted: 1861

KENTUCKY
Adopted: 1792

LOUISIANA
Adopted: 1902

MAINE
Adopted: 1820

MARYLAND
Adopted: 1876

MASSACHUSETTS
Adopted: 1885

MICHIGAN
Adopted: 1835

MINNESOTA
Adopted: 1861

MISSISSIPPI
Adopted: 1798

MISSOURI
Adopted: 1822

MONTANA
Adopted: 1893

NEBRASKA
Adopted: 1867

NEVADA
Adopted: 1866

NEW HAMPSHIRE
Adopted: 1931

NEW JERSEY
Adopted: 1777

NEW MEXICO
Adopted: 1912

NEW YORK
Adopted: 1882

NORTH CAROLINA
Adopted: 1983

NORTH DAKOTA
Adopted: 1863

OHIO
Adopted: 1847, 1996

OKLAHOMA
Adopted: 1905

OREGON
Adopted: 1857

PENNSYLVANIA
Adopted: 1790

RHODE ISLAND
Adopted: 1644

SOUTH CAROLINA
Adopted: 1776

SOUTH DAKOTA
Adopted: 1885

TENNESSEE
Adopted: 1796

TEXAS
Adopted: 1836, 1992

UTAH
Adopted: 1896

VERMONT
Adopted: 1778

VIRGINIA
Adopted: 1776, 1930

WASHINGTON
Adopted: 1889

WEST VIRGINIA
Adopted: 1863

WISCONSIN
Adopted: 1851

WYOMING
Adopted: 1893

Parts of the Great Seal

A seal is an image that represents ownership or originality. State seals are images that reflect the values, beliefs, and history of a state. A **die** is used to imprint the seals on official government documents. The governor of each state has authority over use of the state seal.

SYMBOL Many images on state seals are symbols that represent an idea or belief held by the state. These symbols may be heraldic, which means they take the form of armory. Examples are shields and helmets. Other symbols are mythological, such as goddesses. Images, such as olive branches, represent peace, while oak branches represent strength.

MOTTO Many state seals contain a motto. A motto is a short saying about the people's values or beliefs. Some mottoes on the state seals are in English. Others are in French, Spanish, Greek, or Latin.

DATE Many seals contain dates that are important to the states. These dates might be the date people settled in the area, the date of statehood, or the date the seal was adopted. Some seals have more than one date.

PICTURE Many state seals contain images that portray something important about the state. Pictures of mountains, rivers, and animals show the importance of nature. Farmers and miners represent industry. Each state has carefully chosen pictures that best show what is important to the people and the area.

Test Your Knowledge

1 Which state seals feature the goddess of liberty?

2 What is the eagle on the Great Seal holding in its talons?

3 Which state seal has the word "Sovereignty" upside-down?

4 Which state seal was the only seal designed by a woman?
   a. Colorado
   b. Alabama
   c. Texas
   d. Idaho

5 List four state seals that feature an eagle.

6 What year was the Great Seal adopted?

7 Which seal features a map of the state?
   a. New Hampshire
   b. Alabama
   c. Kentucky
   d. Maine

8 Name three seals that picture American Indian culture.

PASSPORT

United States of America

9 Which state seal displays an anchor?
   a. Rhode Island
   b. Indiana
   c. Virginia
   d. Washington

13 How many times a year is the Great Seal used?

14 Which is the only state seal that has a family coat of arms?

10 What year was the first seal emblem chosen?

15 Who was asked to create the Great Seal?

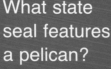

11 Which state has the nickname "Treasure State?"
   a. Connecticut
   b. North Dakota
   c. South Carolina
   d. Montana

12 What state seal features a pelican?

Answers:
1. Arkansas, Hawai'i, New Jersey, New York, and North Carolina
2. an olive branch and arrows
3. Illinois
4. d. Idaho
5. Arkansas, Illinois, Iowa, Michigan, Mississippi, Missouri, New Mexico, New York, Oregon, Pennsylvania, and Utah
6. 1782
7. b. Alabama
8. Florida, Kansas, Massachusetts, Minnesota, and Oklahoma
9. a. Rhode Island
10. 1908, in Illinois
11. d. Montana
12. Louisiana
13. 2,000 to 3,000
14. Maryland
15. Benjamin Franklin, John Adams, and Thomas Jefferson

Create Your Own Seal

Create a seal to represent you. Begin by thinking about what type of seal you want. Use this book to help you. What does the seal of your state look like? Will your design be similar to your state seal? Will it be different? What symbols will you use in your seal? Will you use animals, flowers, trees, or people?

Think about how your seal will look. Will your seal be large or small? Will it have a motto? What symbols will you use? Why? Look at the pictures in this book for help. You can also see the Great Seal and learn the story of how it was created online at **www.greatseal.com**.

Draw your seal on a piece of paper. Use the diagram on pages 42 and 43 to help you design the parts of your seal. Color your drawing with felt markers. When you are finished, label the parts of your seal.

Write a description of your seal. What are the features of your seal? What does it say about you?

Further Research

Many books and websites provide information on state seals. To learn more about seals, borrow books from the library or surf the Internet.

Books

Most libraries have computers that connect to a database for researching information. If you input a key word, you will be provided with a list of books in the library that contain information on that topic. Non-fiction books are arranged numerically, using their call number. Fiction books are organized alphabetically by the author's last name.

Websites

Find fun facts about each of the 50 U.S. states by clicking on this map from the U.S. Census Bureau. **www.census.gov/schools/facts**.

Learn facts and figures about all 50 states by visiting **www.shgresources.com/resources/almanac**.

To discover more about state seals at **www.netstate.com/state_seals.htm**.

Read about the Great Seal of the United States at **www.state.gov/documents/organization/27807.pdf**.

Glossary

die: a tool for imprinting a design

diety: a god or goddess

Great Plains: a vast grassland region covering 10 U.S. states and 4 Canadian provinces. Used for farming and raising cattle

monarchy: when a king or queen rules a country

New England: the most northeastern U.S. states—Connecticut, Rhode Island, Massachusetts, New Hampshire, Vermont, and Maine

perpetuated: to last or be remembered

phoenix: a mythical bird which was thought to live for 500 years, burn itself to death, and then rise from the ashes

reservoir: a lake where water is stored until it is needed

sovereignty: a country's ability to rule itself, free from other powers

Index